GUM GUIDE

COMIC CONVENTION EDITION

exclusive guide for comic convention
trading card collectibles

Paul Hart & Nigel Spill

Introduction

You are holding in your hands our first ever Comic Convention edition of our Gum Guide. This is in response to the many who have requested to publish a guide like this over the years. We have seen more shows and conventions offer trading cards. So many in fact that the need for this guide has arisen.

It is a strong indicator of the strength of the trading card hobby that both big and small manufacturers are feeling the need to be involved in these events. Whether it is a card produced to promote upcoming sets or a full set only available at the event, the choices are strong and fulfilling.

As with our previous guides, every time we think we have it all, we discover something new. We are on a ongoing journey to find the best non sports collectibles around the world!

Acknowledgements

We would like to thank all the companies and individuals for all their dedication in producing their great trading cards. Thanks to Tom at Breygent, Mark at Topps, Steve at Rittenhouse Archives and Cryptozoic for all the invaluable information you have provided us with.

Thank you to Karen Spill for all her hard work and efforts in getting this guide completed.

Most importantly, thanks to you, the collector, for continuing to make collecting trading cards the greatest hobby in the world!

Disclaimer

The Gum Guide Comic Convention guide is not an offer to buy or sell at these prices. As stated, prices are volatile due to market forces. The guide is purely designed as a database of information for collectors.
All images and brand names remain the copyright of the original licensees and are used for reference purposes only.
All rights reserved.

Disclaimer: Information contained in this book is accurate to the best of our knowledge. E.&O.E.

Visit us at: www.spillproductions.com

Product Name	Convention/ Show Name	Description	Unit Price (USD)
108 Stitches	SDCC15	12 card set including Roger Clemens	50
258 West	SDCC10	8 card promo card set TV's stars	40
258 West	SDCC12	3 card MP12-01,02 unum	15
258 West	2012 Wondercon	3 card set	15
258 West	SDCC11	7 card set	10
258 West	SDCC15	5 card set	15
258 West Matt Smith	SDCC13	1 card	10
258 West Matt Smith	2013 Wondercon	1 card	15
5finity Trizia	Chicago Non Sports 2015	1 card	7
8 Bit Zombie	SDCC15	Set of 4 1A-4A	20
9 The Movie	SDCC09	9 card set	25
Abrams Postcards	SDCC16	6 card set including Star Wars	12
Abrams Return of the Jedi	SDCC16	4 card set from book	15
Abrams Star Trek Set	SDCC13	4 card set from book	25
Abrams Bazooka Joe set	SDCC13	4 card set from book	15
Abrams Mars Attacks	SDCC12	4 card set from book	30
Abrams Star Wars	SDCC16	1 card oversized	5
Abrams Trolls	SDCC12	4 card set	8
Acme Ink Dead Ahead	2012 Wondercon	3 card set	12
Age of Darkness	NYCC14	Sketch Card Pack only 300 made	50
Agent Wild	2016 Wondercon	1 card	3
AJ Scudiere	SDCC13	5 card set	22

Product Name	Convention/ Show Name	Description	Unit Price (USD)
Alex Ross Star Wars Bookmark Set	SDCC15	2 card set	12
Alias S3 Preview Set	SDCC04	7 card set	20
Alice in Wonderland Disney Movie	SDCC10	7 card promo set	35
Alien Anthology	SDCC16	Upper Deck Foil Promo Martinez Signed version	35
Aliens Took My Girl	2012 Wondercon	12 card set	40
All Ghouls School	SDCC11	6 card set	35
AM870 The Answer	2014 Wondercon	1 card radio station promo	4
America's Army IDW	SDCC13	Set of 2 plus sketch card	35
Anne Frankenstein	2011 Wondercon	3 card set	10
Anovos Bookmarks	SDCC16	12 bookmark set includes Star Wars and Star Trek	30
Appleseed	SDCC14	4 card set oversized	8
Arby Jr's Pets	2014	6 card set	8
Archies The Art of Betty and Veronica	SDCC13	1 card	4
Armageddon Hell	2013 Comikaze	4 card set	12
Art Hustle	SDCC11	2 card set	20
Art Hustle	SDCC12	5 card set	22
Art Hustle	SDCC10	1 promo card	3
Art Hustle	SDCC13	1 card	4
Art Hustle Chase Set	SDCC10	6 card set autographed	150
Art of Jov	2015 Comikaze	2 card set	6
Artbox 24	SDCC08	3 card set	15
Artbox Harry Potter	SDCC09	2 promo card set	12
Artbox Lost	SDCC09	5 card set	20
Artgasm	SDCC11	4 card set	6
Avatar Animated	SDCC06	6 card set	25

Product Name	Convention/ Show Name	Description	Unit Price (USD)
Avengers	NYCC15	Sideshow Promo gift card	9
AVP Movie	Convention	3 card set	20
Baby Daddy	2015 D23	3 card set	15
Back to the Future	SDCC14	Like Topps numbered 89-98	45
Back to the Future	SDCC15	Lenticular card postcard size	30
Batman	NYCC15	Sideshow promo gift card	5
Batman Action Figures Set	SDCC15	22 card set	200
Batman Bookmark	2014 Comikaze	1 bookmark card	3
Batman DC	SDCC16	Uncut sheet of 9 cards	15
Batman Foil Promos	SDCC16	9 card set DC8-19	50
Batman/Predator	Promotional	8 card set DC/Dark Horse	40
Battleborn 2K	Convention	23/25 in packs other 2 cards in game + 6 puzzle cards	30
Battlestar Galactica Cylon	SDCC13	1 card	40
Bear and Nightingale	SDCC16	3 card set	10
Beerus Panini	SDCC16	Promo card	10
Belles War	SDCC14	2 card set	6
Benchwarmers	SDCC14	9 card set	20
Benchwarmers Dreamgirls	SDCC15	Set of 5 1-5 plus A1-4 Auto cards	50
Benchwarmers Kickstarter	SDCC15	5 card set	35
Benchwarmers Super Heroes	SDCC15	9 card set	40

Product Name	Convention/ Show Name	Description	Unit Price (USD)
Best Buy Jurassic World	2015	8 card set	20
Bettie Page	SDCC11	3 card set	200
Billy Dee	2014 Wondercon	5 card set	12
Black Mask Studios	SDCC16	5 card set	15
Black Wrath	2014 Wondercon	1 card	6
Blackish	2015 D23	1 card	8
Blade Raiders	SDCC12	2 card set	10
Blindspot	Promotional	Promo card	10
Blood Sucka Jones	2014 Comikaze	6 card set	10
Bob Burden Flaming Carrot	SDCC13	20 card set	100
Bob Burden Mysterians	SDCC11	20 card set	75
Bob's Burgers	2015 Comikaze	1 card	5
Bob's Burgers Stickers	2015 Comikaze	5 sticker card set	15
Bombshells DC	SDCC16	Uncut sheet of 9 cards	15
Bombshells Women of War	2012 Wondercon	1 card	5
Bottom of the Ninth	SDCC12	5 card set	40
Brave Movie	Promotional	Subway 6 card 3D Set	35
Breaking Dawn Pt 2	SDCC12	15 card set	25
Breygent American Horror Story	SDCC13	1 card	5
Breygent American Horror Story	SDCC14	8 card set	40
Breygent American Horror Story	Philly Non Sports 2015	1 card	4
Breygent American Horror Story Props and Autographs	SDCC14	Various autographs and props	Varies
Breygent American Horror Story Props and Autographs	SDCC16	Various	Varies

Product Name	Convention/ Show Name	Description	Unit Price (USD)
Breygent Bates Motel	Philly Non Sports 2015	1 card	4
Breygent Bates Motel	Chicago Non Sports 2015	1 card	6
Breygent Dawn	SDCC12	1 card	3
Breygent Deadworld Set	NYCC12	7 card set	10
Breygent Dexter	SDCC12	3 card set	12
Breygent Dexter	SDCC15	2 card set	10
Breygent Dexter	Philly Non Sports 2015	2 card set	8
Breygent Dexter	Chicago Non Sports 2012	1 card	5
Breygent Dexter Props and Autographs	SDCC12	Various singles	Varies
Breygent Grimm	SDCC11	4 card set	15
Breygent Grimm	SDCC12	2 card set	6
Breygent Grimm	NYCC12	4 card promo set	10
Breygent Grimm	Philly Non Sports 2016	2 card set	6
Breygent Grumpy Cat	SDCC16	7 card set	10
Breygent Grumpy Cat Promo	SDCC16	1 card	10
Breygent Jimi Hendrix	SDCC12	1 card	20
Breygent Jurassic	SDCC15	2 card set	10
Breygent Jurassic Dom	Philly Non Sports 2015	1 card	3
Breygent Night of the Living Dead	SDCC12	1 card	10
Breygent Red Sonja	SDCC12	1 card	10
Breygent Vampirella	SDCC12	1 card	10
Breygent Vampirella	SDCC12	Various autographs and sketches	Varies

Product Name	Convention/ Show Name	Description	Unit Price (USD)
Breygent War Lord of Mars	SDCC12	Various autographs and sketches	Varies
Breygent War Lord of Mars	SDCC12	2 card set	10
Breygent War Lord of Mars	Chicago Non Sports 2012	2 card set	10
Breygent Women of Dynamite	Philly Non Sports 2015	1 card	3
Breygent World of Fantaxy	NYCC12	1 card	3
Breygent/Deadworld	SDCC12	Various autographed cards	Varies
Breygent Vampirella	SDCC11	1 card	10
Brotherhood Movie	Cineworld	6 card postcard set	15
Buffy Dark Horse	SDCC07	8 card set	15
Buffy Fan Club	SDCC00	4 card set	20
Bunk'd	2015 D23	1 card	6
Butcher Baker	SDCC12	1 card	4
Capcon	SDCC08	3 card set	9
Capstone Super Hero Bookmarks	SDCC13	4 bookmark card set	11
Captain Marvel Card Set	SDCC16	Kris Anka signed card 1 of 8	20
Carl's Jr X Men	2014	9 card set	20
Cartamundi	2015 Star Wars Celebration	4 card set	25
CBLDF	SDCC11	1 card set	3
CBS NCIS	SDCC11	4 card set	20
CCAS	2012 Wondercon	4 card set	10
Celebrity Autographs	Promotional	Andy Buckle Various film/tv/pop 14 different known	Varies
Chara 10th Anniversary	SDCC16	3 card set oversized	10
Chevy Trading Cards	2013 Auto Show (Los Angeles)	16 card set	20

Product Name	Convention/ Show Name	Description	Unit Price (USD)
Chicago Show	2004	22 card set of various signers	60
Chicago Show	2003	18 card set of various signers	70
Chicago Show	2010	17 card set of various signers	50
Chocolate Milk Benchwarmers	2015	1 card	15
Chris Riff Star Wars	2016 Star Wars Celebration	8 card Star Wars Art Set	25
Cinequest Femme Fatales	SDCC12	2 card set	4
Clone Wars Hunter Set	SDCC10	4 card set	5
Comic Book All Stars	SDCC16	26 card set	45
Coveted	SDCC12	3 card set	10
Creepy cards	NYCC15	3 card pack	10
Cryptozoiac Castle TV Show	SDCC12	P3 exclusive promo card	10
Cryptozoiac Gotham GTS	Philly Non Sports 2016	1 card	35
Cryptozoiac Toy Promo Card Set	SDCC16	12 card set	40
Cryptozoiac Batman	SDCC15	1 card	15
Cryptozoiac Batman	SDCC16	9 card set	100
Cryptozoiac DC New 52	2012 Comikaze	1 card	15
Cryptozoiac Fringe Hand	SDCC15	1 card	20
Cryptozoiac Fringe Seahorse	SDCC15	1 card	20
Cryptozoiac Penny Dreadful	SDCC15	1 card	18
Cryptozoiac The Walking Dead P3	SDCC12	1 promo card	15
Cyclops Disney Art	2015 D23	12 card set	100
Cyclops Disney Art	SDCC16	3 card set	25
Dan Vs.	SDCC11	4 card set	10
Daredevil S2	Promotional	5 card set	15
Dark Horse Dark Siders II	SDCC12	4 card set	40

Product Name	Convention/ Show Name	Description	Unit Price (USD)
Dark Legacy The Rising	SDCC13	4 card set	8
Dashner Army 3D	SDCC14	1 card	10
Dawn of the Planet of the Apes	SDCC14	1 card	10
DC Girls	SDCC16	9 card set	15
DC Martian Manhunter	SDCC16	1 card	8
DC Superhero Girls	SDCC16	8 card set	50
DD Art	2016 Wondercon	12 card set including Star Wars, Walking Dead and more	35
Dead Speed	SDCC14	6 card set	10
Dead Speed	SDCC09	10 card set	8
Dead Tired Zombie Hunter	SDCC13	1 card	4
Deadworld	SDCC15	2 card set	10
Despicable Me 2	SDCC13	1 card	5
Dexter	SDCC09	6 card set	30
Dexter S4	NYCC12	Foil promo card	10
Dexter S4	SDCC13	3 card set	15
Dick Grayson	2016 Wondercon	1 business card	6
Dire Wolf	SDCC16	2 different promo cards	15
Disney Big Hero 6	2014 Comikaze	6 card set	15
Disney Brave	2012 Book Fair	8 postcard set	8
Disney Coasters	2015 D23	4 coaster set from Disney music	40
Disney Fine Art Bookmarks	2013 D23	16 bookmark card set	75
Disney Fine Art Bookmarks	2015 D23	21 bookmark card set	100
Disney Fine Art Collectors Edition	2015 D23	4 card set	15
Disney Star Wars Rebels	2015 Star Wars Celebration	1 card	8
Disney Store Star Wars Force Awakens	2015	8 card set	50
Disney Store Star Wars US Series 1	2014	9 card set	12

Product Name	Convention/ Show Name	Description	Unit Price (USD)
Disney Store Star Wars US Series 2	2014	6 card set	10
Disney Store Star Wars US Series 3	2014	6 card set	20
Disney Studios Collectors Card Sample Pack	2013 D23	7 card set	60
Disneyland Diamond Celebration	2015 D23	9 card set	40
DK Disney Finding Dory Bookmark	SDCC16	1 card	5
DK Star Wars Bookmark	SDCC12	4 bookmark card set	10
DK Star Wars Bookmark	SDCC15	4 bookmark card set	10
DK Star Wars Rey Bookmark	SDCC16	1 bookmark	5
Dr. Grordborts	SDCC08	6 card set	10
Dr. Who Topps	SDCC16	Oversized card set 1-30	100
Dr. Who	BBC	Small lenticular card set of 32. Issued randomly in micro figures. Very scarce!	400
Dr. Who Time Twisters	Promotional	4 card set	15
Dr. Who Fandom	Promotional	9 card set. Only 100 made	30
Dr. Who Inkworks	SDCC07	6 card set	30
Dr. Who Con	SDCC16	1 card	5
Dog with a Blog	2015 D23	1 card	10
Dorothy of Oz	SDCC10	9 card promo set	50
Dragonseed and Earthtribe	SDCC09	6 card set	15
Dreamworks	SDCC13	6 card set	32
Droid Builders Set	2016 Star Wars Celebration	25 card set 100 sets issued	250
Eclipse	Promotional	5 card folder set	30
Eclipse	Promotional	2010 Holiday Exclusive Card. 500 made	10

Product Name	Convention/ Show Name	Description	Unit Price (USD)
Eclipse	Promotional	Masterpieces 11 card set	30
Eclipse	Promotional	Twilightgraphs 20 card set	45
Eclipse	Promotional	Foil Set 1. 10 card set	30
Eclipse	Promotional	Foil Set 2. 10 card set	30
EFX	SDCC12	9 card set Film/TV	50
EL Sonador	SDCC16	1 card	3
Emerald	SDCC11	4 card set	5
Emerald Atlas	SDCC13	4 card set	4
End Game	SDCC14	14 card set	12
Eve	SDCC15	1 card	4
Everybody Wants Some	2016 Wondercon	1 card	3
Ewok Builders Club	2015 Star Wars Celebration	12 card set	100
Factory	SDCC10	6 card set includes Beatles	12
Factory The Prisoner Village Map	SDCC10	9 card set	50
Fanboy of the Universe	SDCC11	1 card	3
Fanboy of the Universe	SDCC13	1 card	3
Fandango Now	SDCC16	13 card set	75
Fandango Now Sideshow	SDCC16	3 gift card set	20
Farscape	Convention	Watch Farscape 6 card set	20
Femme Fatales	2012 Wondercon	22 card set	50
Femme Fatales Season 1 & 2	SDCC12	5 card set PR1-5 plus 2 promos FFP1, P2	35
Firefly Online	SDCC15	1 card	8
Force United	2015 Star Wars Celebration	6 card set	10

Product Name	Convention/ Show Name	Description	Unit Price (USD)
Fox Animation Throwdown	SDCC16	5 card set	25
Fringe	SDCC09	3 card set. Feather, Frog, Seahorse	25
Frompie	2015 Promotional	4 card set	12
Frozen Anna and Elsa	2015 D23	4 card set	10
Frozen Olaf	2015 D23	9 card set	35
Funimation	SDCC13	5 card anime set	30
FX Now	SDCC15	9 card tv promo set	50
G-Force	SDCC09	8 card set	10
Gamers Guide	2015 D23	1 card	6
Garbage Pail Kids Topps	NYCC15	Basuritas 5 x 7 10 card set	20
Gentle Giant	SDCC16	11 card set Star Wars, Marvel, etc	35
Gentle Giant	SDCC15	10 card set Star Wars, Marvel, etc	25
Ghostbusters	IMAX	Edwards Irvine Cinema Limited Edition of 500	5
GI Joe Finest	2014 Wondercon	5 card set	10
Girls of Snake and Mongoose Movie	SDCC13	6 card set	15
Gladiator Models	Furuta, Japan	8 card set	45
Glenn Morshower	NYCC	Limited Edition signed trading card	20
Gotham	SDCC14	Lenticular Card	10
Gotham Playing Cards	SDCC16	Promotional boxed set	25
Gravity Falls	SDCC15	3 card set	100
Gravo-4	2012 Wondercon	1 card	5
Grey Walker Novels	SDCC12	9 card set	35
Grid Traveller	2015 Wondercon	15 card set	30

Product Name	Convention/ Show Name	Description	Unit Price (USD)
Grimm Fairy Tales	Philly Non Sports 2016	1 card	3
Guardians of the Galaxy Marvel Now	SDCC13	6 card set Ironman short printed	20
Guardians of the Galaxy	SDCC15	6 card set	5
Hacktivity	2014 Comikaze	2 card set	5
Hannah Lynn	SDCC16	Poppy promo card	5
Hannah Lynn	SDCC15	promo card	5
Hannah Lynn	SDCC14	promo card	5
Hannah Lynn	SDCC13	promo card	5
Hanzo	SDCC16	1 card	3
Harry Houdini	Chicago Non Sports 2012	1 promo card	5
Harry Potter Dumbledor's Army	SDCC10	5 sets of 4 oversize costume card sets – 50 of each only issued by Artbox	200
Hasbro Diorama Workshop	2015 Star Wars Celebration	6 card set	20
Haven Audrey Parker 3d	SDCC13	1 card	10
Haven Business Cards	SDCC14	2 card set	15
Hawaii 5-0	SDCC10	1 promo card	3
Hello Kitty Upper Deck	SDCC16	6 oversized card set	40
Hello Kitty Con Bookmark Set	2014 Hello Kitty Con	2 card set	8
Hello Kitty Con Welcome Card	2014 Hello Kitty Con	1 card	5
Hello Kitty Upper Deck	2014 Hello Kitty Con	6 oversized card set	45
Hello Kitty Con Spam	2014 Hello Kitty Con	1 card	12
Hero	2014 Wondercon	6 card set	8

Product Name	Convention/ Show Name	Description	Unit Price (USD)
Hero Game	SDCC15	4 card set	10
Heroes of X Box	Convention	Combat cards box set	15
Heroes Season 1	SDCC06	4 card set	10
Heroes Tattoos	SDCC09	6 card set	10
Holly G School Bites	SDCC13	1 card	4
Horrible Monster	SDCC12	1 card	3
House of Anubis	Promotional	10 card character set	35
How to Train Your Dragon 2	SDCC14	1 card	4
How to Train Your Dragon 2	2014 Wondercon	1 card	10
Hunger Games Auction	SDCC13	6 card set	30
Ichabod Jones	2015 Wondercon	5 card set	20
IDW Back to the Future	SDCC15	1 card	15
IDW Limited Bookmarks	SDCC12	6 card set	15
IDW Locke and Key	2012 Wondercon	9 card set	35
IDW Mars Attacks	Promotional	100-card set. Only 250 made.	400
IDW Smoke and Mirrors	2012 Wondercon	5 card set	10
IDW Smoke and Mirrors	SDCC12	1 card	5
Image Patience	SDCC12	1 card	4
IMDB Dossier Series	SDCC16	30-card set. TV and film stars	250
Infex	SDCC12	Series 1 – 5 cards + 1 sticker	10
Infex	SDCC12	Series 2 – 5 cards + 1 sticker	10
Infex	SDCC12	Series 3 – 5 cards + 1 sticker	10
Inkworks	SDCC08	4 card promo set	10

Product Name	Convention/ Show Name	Description	Unit Price (USD)
Inkworks Ghost Whisperer	SDCC09	6 card promo set	15
Invictus	2015 Wondercon	4 card set	6
Iron Dead Legends	Philly Non Sports 2016	1 card	3
Iron Man Stark Industries	SDCC09	4 business card set	25
Jane and the Dragon	SDCC08	4 card set	15
Jason Chalker Manly Art	2013 Comikaze	18-card set. Multiple characters	50
Jason Chalker Manly Art Star Wars Toy Set	2013 Comikaze	18 card set	50
Jason Chalker Manly Art Star Wars Set	2013 Comikaze	18 card set	50
Jedi Temple Kenner Set	2016 Star Wars Celebration	4 card set	35
Jennifer's Body	SDCC09	2 card set	12
Jessie	2015 D23	1 card	10
John Constantine	SDCC14	Business card	15
John Wayne	SDCC05	1 card	10
Justice League Tarot	SDCC15	1 card	12
Justin Chung	SDCC08-15	Various promos	5
K-Scary	SDCC10	1 card	3
KC Undercover	2015 D23	1 card	6
Kaidoz	SDCC11	7 card set	25
Kaidoz Animals	SDCC13	12 card set	20
Kingdom Keepers	SDCC13	6 card set	10
Kingdom Keepers	2015 D23	1 card	7
Kirby Buckets	2015 D23	1 card	8
Komodo Den	2015 Wondercon	2 card set	10
Konami Star Wars Force Collection	2015 Star Wars Celebration	5 card set	15
Lab Rats	2015 D23	1 card	7
Ladies of the Spirit	SDCC08	5 card set	20
Legend of the Seeker	2012 Wondercon	12 card set	40

Product Name	Convention/ Show Name	Description	Unit Price (USD)
Legend of the Seeker	2013 Wondercon	5 card set	45
Legends of Orkney	SDCC15	1 card	10
Lego Nexo Knights	SDCC16	1 bookmark	3
Liv and Maddie	2015 D23	1 card	6
Lord of the Rings	SDCC08	52 playing card set	50
Lost Girl The Wanderer	SDCC13	1 card	20
Lost Season 1	MEM	L1 – MS UK Exclusive Promo	10
Lost The Dharma Initiative	SDCC06	6 card set	15
Lucifer Playing Cards	SDCC16	Promotional Boxed Set	25
M & M's 75th Anniversary	SDCC16	12 card set	25
Magic Adventures	Promotional	8 card set	15
Magic the Gathering Donato Collection	SDCC12	1 card	20
Magic the Gathering Spellslingers	2015 Wondercon	1 card	5
Mars Attacks Topps	NYCC12	Exclusive Show Sketch Card	99
Mars Attacks Invasion Topps	SDCC14	9 card set	35
Mars Attacks Topps	SDCC12	9 card set	50
Marvel A Force	SDCC16	G Willow signed card 1 of 8	20
Marvel Avengers Upper Deck	SDCC11	9 card set	10
Marvel Coasters	2016 Wondercon	6 coaster card set. Ironman, etc.	25
Marvel Original Sin	SDCC14	1 card oversize	5
Marvel Rocket Raccoon	SDCC14	1 card oversize	7
Marvel Star Wars Poe Dameron	SDCC16	1 card oversize	5
Marvel Super Heroes	Exhibition	13 card set	45

Product Name	Convention/ Show Name	Description	Unit Price (USD)
Marvel Universe	SDCC11	9 card set SD1-9	30
Marvin the Magician	SDCC13	1 card	3
Mickey Mouse and Oswald 3D	SDCC14	1 card oversize	25
Mighty Med	2015 D23	1 card	8
Miles from Tomorrowland	2015 D23	1 card	3
Minds Eye TV Show	NEC UK	9 card set	25
Monster School Movie	SDCC13	Set of 22 cards. #8 not issued	35
Monsters HD	SDCC04	12 card set	50
Monsters vs. Aliens	SDCC08	8 card set	10
Monsterwax Dinosaur Galaxy	Philly Non Sport 2015	4 card set	6
Mortal Instruments Tattoo Set	SDCC13	6 card set	15
Mouse Heart	SDCC16	5 card set	6
My Emo Vortex	2015 Wondercon	6 card set	12
My Little Pony	NYCC	F37 foil card	Spec
My Little Pony	NYCC	Toys R Us 13 card set	15
My Little Pony	NYCC13	Princess Luna Foil Card F45	25
My Little Pony DJ	NYCC13	F41 Exclusive Promo Card	25
My Little Pony F41 Foil	NYCC13	1 card	10
My Little Pony Pinkie Pie	SDCC15	1 card	12
My Little Pony Princess Luna	NYCC13	1 card	20
Mystery Team	SDCC09	15 card set	20
Naruto	2012 Wondercon	7 card set	25
Naruto Ultimate Ninja Storm 3	2013 Wondercon	4 card set	15
Ndbag The Bogeyman	SDCC16	4 card set	10
Ndbag The Bogeyman	SDCC15	4 card set	10
Ndbag The Bogeyman	SDCC14	4 card set	10

Product Name	Convention/ Show Name	Description	Unit Price (USD)
Ndbag The Bogeyman	SDCC13	4 card set	10
Ndbag The Bogeyman	SDCC12	4 card set	10
Ndbag The Bogeyman	SDCC11	4 card set	10
Ndbag The Bogeyman	SDCC10	4 card set	10
Ndbag The Bogeyman	SDCC09	4 card set	10
Nerdist	2015 Wondercon	4 card set	10
Never More Alice	Chicago Non Sports 2012	1 card	4
New Crusaders	SDCC12	5 card set	35
New Moon	Promotional	2010 Holiday Exclusive Card. 500 made.	10
News World Papers	SDCC14	1 card	5
Nicktoons	SDCC10	5 card set	20
Nightmare Before Christmas Disney	SDCC	Blue Ray/DVD 5 card set	40
Nintendo Pokedex	SDCC11	1 card	10
Norwich Star Wars Club	2007 Star Wars Celebration	24 card set	40
Obama Nation	SDCC09	1 card	5
Official Pix Star Wars	SDCC09	Set unknown amount	20
Oswald Chronicles	SDCC09	1 card	5
Outcast TV Show	SDCC16	81 card set plus random printing plates in box	85
Pachuko Boy	SDCC09	6 card set	10
Pacific Rim	2013 Wondercon	5 card set	50
Panini Dragon Ball Z	SDCC14	5 card set	200
Panini Dragon Ball Z	SDCC15	3 card set	50
Panini Dragon Ball Z Beeruz	SDCC16	1 card	10
Pantalones Texas	2013 Comikaze	1 card	5
Papercuts WWE	SDCC14	4 card set	20
Passage	SDCC12	Set (unknown)	varies

Product Name	Convention/ Show Name	Description	Unit Price (USD)
Peanuts	Promotional	13 card cast set	30
Philly Show Promos	Philly Non Sports	88 card set. Various dealers, manufacturers and celebrities	varies
PHL 17	Promotional	Set (unknown)	20
Pink Girl The Scone	SDCC12	9 card set	45
Pixar Short Films	SDCC	Cello pack set	20
Planet of Apes Conspiracy	SDCC11	10 card set 1-9 + 0 card	75
Playroom Female Bunny	SDCC13	2 card set	6
Poe Dameron	SDCC16	Game promo card	5
Pokemon	SDCC08	1 promo card	15
Pokemon	SDCC09	1 promo card	12
Pokemon Aipon	SDCC10	1 promo card	10
Polychrome	SDCC15	4 card set	10
Poohs Heffalump Movie	Promotional	9 card promo set, puzzle back	35
Popzilla	SDCC15	1 card	5
Power Rangers	SDCC13	7 card set	65
Power Rangers Galaxy	2015 Wondercon	1 card	3
Power Rangers Unite	SDCC15	6 card set	25
Presidential Monsters	SDCC11	3 card set	15
Pretty Little Liars	2015 D23	1 card	10
Private Maid	2016 Anime Expo	1 card	10
Private Maid	SDCC16	1 card	10
Punk Rock	NYCC12	3 card set	10
R2D2 Builders Club	2015 Star Wars Celebration	7 card set, 1 is very rare	100
Random House Star Wars Set	SDCC11	3 card set	12
Ratatouille Movie	Convention	6 scratch and sniff promo card set	30
Ray Harryhausen	Furuta Models Japan	10 card set	75
RC Harvey	SDCC16	1 card	5

Product Name	Convention/ Show Name	Description	Unit Price (USD)
The Reconcilers	SDCC11	5 card set	20
Red	SDCC10	6 card set	8
Red Sonja	MEM11	UK Exclusive Promo	8
Reel Icons	Convention	Rachel Smith Promo Card	10
Reelz XXIII	SDCC12	Ghostbusters 3 card set	6
Renegade Destiny Aurora Chronicles	2015 Comikaze	3 card set	10
Rescue Bots	SDCC11	Sheet of 4 cards	10
Resident Evil	Promotional	Outbreak Set by Capcom	25
Riddick	SDCC13	1 card	5
Rittenhouse	SDCC10	5 card promo set	12
Rittenhouse	SDCC12	5 card promo set	10
Rittenhouse Continuum	Chicago Non Sports 2015	1 card	5
Rittenhouse Continuum	SDCC13	1 card	4
Rittenhouse Eureka	SDCC11	1 card	5
Rittenhouse Falling Skies	SDCC13	1 card	4
Rittenhouse Game of Thrones	Philly Non Sports 2016	2 card set	5
Rittenhouse James Bond 007	Philly Non Sports 2016	1 card	5
Rittenhouse Mavel Puzzle Set	SDCC112	9 card set	20
Rittenhouse Star Trek	SDCC13	1 card	5
Rittenhouse Star Trek Heroes and Villains	Philly Non Sports 2016	1 card	4
Rittenhouse Star Trek Voyager	Philly Non Sports 2016	1 card	5
Rittenhouse Stargate Heroes	SDCC09	1 card	4
Rittenhouse The Avengers Silver Age	Philly Non Sports 2016	1 card	4

Product Name	Convention/ Show Name	Description	Unit Price (USD)
Rittenhouse True Blood	SDCC13	1 card	4
Rittenhouse Under the Dome	Philly Non Sports 2016	1 card	3
Rittenhouse Warehouse 13	SDCC13	1 card	4
Rittenhouse Warehouse 13	SDCC11	1 card	5
Rittenhouse Women of Marvel	SDCC13	1 card	4
Rittenhouse Star Trek	SDCC09	1 card	8
Rizzoli and Isles	SDCC10	1 card	4
Robert Aragon	SDCC12	4 card set	20
Rocket Boy Sticker Set	2014	5 promo card set	12
RR Parks The Three Stooges	Chicago Non Sports 2015	1 card	4
RR Parks The Three Stooges	Philly Non Sports 2016	1 card	3
Rusty Blades	SDCC12	1 card	4
S is for Ska	2015 Wondercon	3 card set	12
Sanctum 3D	SDCC14	1 card	5
Sandy Lion Star Wars 3D Set	Promotional	15 card set	60
Scarabs	2012 Comikaze	3 card set	20
School of Fear	SDCC10	4 card set	5
Scorpion	SDCC14	6 card set	40
Scott Harben	SDCC12	Marvel/Film Cards (ongoing)	8
Scott Harben	SDCC	Series of 30 cards issues over several years	75
Scratch 9	2015 Comikaze	9 card set	20
Screen Used	SDCC12	4 card set blue 1 bonus card (5) series 1	50
SCTV	SDCC	8 card set	25
See Studio Blue Shift	SDCC10	3 card set	8
Septinus Heap	SDCC14	9 card set	5
Serenity	SDCC05	SP-SD	5

Product Name	Convention/ Show Name	Description	Unit Price (USD)
Seth Says	SDCC14	1 card	3
Shatner O War	SDCC15	8 card set	20
She That Kills The Dead	2015 Wondercon	2 card set	8
Sherrilyn Kenyon	SDCC13-15	Various Cards with variants	5
Sherrilyn Kenyon	SDCC14	19 card set	50
Sherrilyn Kenyon	SDCC15	8 card set	20
Sherrilyn Kenyon	SDCC16	13 card set	50
Sherrilyn Kenyon	SDCC13	10 card set	45
Snow White and the Huntsman Movie	NEC MEM	Factory sealed set	15
Sicario Movie	SDCC15	5 card set	15
Sidekick	NYCC11	Tandem promo card	10
Sidekick Promo	NYCC11	1 card	10
Sidekick Tarzan	Philly Non Sports 2016	1 card	3
Silly Symphony Collection	2015 D23	3 card set	35
Sin-Jin Smyth	Convention	7 card set	25
Sinister 3D	SDCC12	1 card	5
Sky Captain and the World of the Tomorrow	Promotional	8 card set	25
Skyfall Series	SDCC16	2 oversized card set	5
Snoopy Belle Girl	SDCC14	6 card set	30
Snow White and the Huntsmen	Promotional	4 promo card set	10
Snuggy Bear	Promotional	1 card	5
Sofia the First	2015 D23	1 card	5
Softball	SDCC16	1 card	3
Soul Hunters	SDCC15	1 card	4
Space Chimps	SDCC08	6 card set	12
Spartacus Blood and Sand	SDCC09	12 card foil set by Starz	45
Spectrum Fillion	SDCC16	5 card set	25
Speed Racer	SDCC11	6 card set plus sketch card	50
Stan Lee Sports Ball	2012 Comikaze	8 card set	38
Stan Lee Super Heroes Ball Wars	2013 Comikaze	2 card set	15

Product Name	Convention/ Show Name	Description	Unit Price (USD)
Stan Lee Zodiac	SDCC15	8 card set	12
Star Cards	Convention	11 different supermegafest	75
Star Trek	SDCC11	USS Enterprise Lenticular Card	10
Star Trek	Philly Non Sports 2016	1 card	5
Star Trek	SDCC16	Rittenhouse 50 artists 50 years factory set	75
Star Trek	Promotional	Mego Star Trek by Gyori (8)	45
Star Trek	Promotional	Into Darkness movie cards – uncut 9 card sheet	40
Star Trek Game Cards	SDCC11	1 card	25
Star Trek	SDCC09	1 lenticular card	8
Star Trek Ladies of the Fleet	SDCC11	7 card set	50
Star Wars ANA Airlines	2016 Star Wars Celebration	1 card	6
Star Wars	2016 Star Wars Celebration	12 regular plus 3 rare foils issued by Konami	45
Star Wars	Glico	Japanese 50 card lenticular set	150
Star Wars	Popitas	9 card foil set from Spain	30
Star Wars	Disney Store UK	12 card Empire Strikes Back foil card set	40
Star Wars	Disney Store UK	12 card Return of the Jedi foil card set	40
Star Wars	Romanian 2015	72 octagonal card set	50
Star Wars	Kent Turkey	48 wrap around small sticker set	50
Star Wars	Japan	The Force Fire Prism Card Set of 20	60

Product Name	Convention/ Show Name	Description	Unit Price (USD)
Star Wars	Japan Kirin Coffee	Force Awakens 20 sticker set	30
Star Wars	Japan Chico Wafers	72 character drawings stickers	75
Star Wars	SDCC05	Darth Vader Card THQ Wireless	10
Star Wars	Promotional	Fandom 9 card Set UK Only 100 sets	30
Star Wars	SDCC09	Star Wars Made Me This Way	5
Star Wars	SDCC16	Topps Oversize 7 different sets	200
Star Wars	2016 Star Wars Celebration	Topps Force Attacks Oversize 8 card set	40
Star Wars	Ficello	6 card set	45
Star Wars	Disney Store UK	12 cards New Hope Foil Card set	40
Star Wars	Kent Turkey	54 Rogue 1 sticker set – Medium Size	30
Star Wars	SDCC	Old Republic Lenticular Card	10
Star Wars	NYCC15	BB-8 Die Cut Stand Up Card	5
Star Wars Action News	SDCC15	Unknown	50
Star Wars Action News	2015 Star Wars Celebration	1 card	15
Star Wars Andy Duke	2016 Star Wars Collection	3 card set in old Topps Style	15
Star Wars BB8 Builders	2016 Star Wars Collection	Matt Denton and Josh Lee #1	5
Star Wars Big Little Golden Book	2015 D23	6 card set	6

Product Name	Convention/ Show Name	Description	Unit Price (USD)
Star Wars Card Trader BB8	SDCC16	1 card	4
Star Wars Card Trader Large	SDCC16	5 card set	25
Star Wars Disney Days	2015 Star Wars Celebration	5 card set	100
Star Wars Celebration Sticker	2015 Wondercon	1 card	15
Star Wars Coasters	SDCC14	4 coaster set	15
Star Wars Crucible Bookmark Set	SDCC13	3 bookmark card set	10
Star Wars Day	SDCC94	Oversized 2 cards	45
Star Wars DC Area Collecting Club	2015 Star Wars Celebration	40 card set	200
Star Wars DK Set	2016 Star Wars Celebration	4 card set	10
Star Wars Fan Fun Day	Norwich Club	18 card set	100
Star Wars Japan	2015 Star Wars Celebration	4 card set	25
Star Wars McQuarrie	SDCC14	6 card set	10
Star Wars Mini Pix Set	2015 Star Wars Celebration	35 card set	60
Star Wars Mint In The Box	2016 Star Wars Celebration	3 card set	25
Star Wars Mint in the Box	2015 Star Wars Celebration	4 card set	35
Star Wars Norwich Set	2016 Star Wars Celebration	3 oversized card set	10
Star Wars Origami	SDCC14	8 card set	6
Star Wars Planete Set	2016 Star Wars Celebration	3 oversized card set	15
Star Wars R2 Builders Club	2016 Star Wars Celebration	26-card set. Only 100 made.	200
Star Wars R2 Builders Club Thin Version	2016 Star Wars Celebration	9 card set	40
Star Wars R2D2 Builders Club	2015 Star Wars Celebration	7 card set	75
Star Wars Rebels XD	2015 D23	1 card	12

Product Name	Convention/ Show Name	Description	Unit Price (USD)
Star Wars Teekay-421	2016 Star Wars Celebration	3 card set	8
Star Wars The Art of Ralph McQuarrie	2015 Star Wars Celebration	Unknown	100
Star Wars Top Trumps Limited Edition	2016 Star Wars Celebration	6 card set	30
Star Wars Topps Spaceship Set	2016 Star Wars Celebration	6 card set	10
Star Wars Trader App	SDCC15	5 oversize cards	25
Star Wars Ultimate Studio Edition	SDCC16	7 card set	35
Star Wars Universe	2016 Star Wars Celebration	3 card set tea time, tourist scum, queens	15
Star Wars Vintage Rebellion	2016 Star Wars Celebration	6 card set	30
Star Wars X-Wing Poedameron	SDCC16	1 card	8
Stealing Home	Promotional	Jodie Foster Movie Promo Set (6)	40
Steam Queens	2014 Wondercon	1 card	6
Steam Queens	2015 Wondercon	1 card	4
Steam Royals	2015 Comikaze	1 card	4
Steam Royals	SDCC15	1 card	5
Stitchers	2015 D23	1 card	8
Street Fighter 2	SDCC16	Udon Set of 4 metal cards	75
Street Fighter Ono	SDCC16	Signed gold metal card	250
Stuart Little	Promotional	Break Cake 3 card set	20
Studs Lego Builders	SDCC12	P1, P2	10
Studs Lego Cards	SDCC12	4 cards	25
Subway Star Wars Rebels	2014	6 card set	20
Suckadelic Lands on Wars	NYC12	3 card set	10
Suckadelic Toy Lords	SDCC13	1 card	5

Product Name	Convention/ Show Name	Description	Unit Price (USD)
Suicide Squad	SDCC16	4 card set in case- only 10 set issues per day.	45
Super 7	SDCC12	8 card set in wax wrapper	40
Super Grammar	SDCC11	5 card set	10
Supergirl DC	SDCC16	Martian Manhunter foil card	10
Superheroes Squad Show	SDCC10	52 card set	15
Superman	SDCC13	Collecting Superman Promo card	10
Superman Man of Steel	2013 Carls Jr	9 card set	25
Switched at Birth	2015 D23	2 card set	10
Tales of Midnight	NEC UK	14 promo card set	25
Target Star Wars Add on Set	2015	3 card set	10
Teddy and the Yeti	SDCC12	3 card set	4
Teddy and the Yeti	SDCC16	1 card	3
Teddy Scares	SDCC16	12 card set	20
Teen Beach Movie 2	2015 D23	1 card	15
Teenage Mutant Ninja Turtles	SDCC13	5 card set	25
Teenage Mutant Ninja Turtles	2014 Comikaze	6 card set	15
Terra Nova	SDCC11	1 card	5
The 4400 TV Show	SDCC06	4 card set	10
The Art of Tim Shay	SDCC13	4 card set	30
The Awesomes TV	SDCC13	8 card set	15
The Bear and The Nightingale	SDCC16	3 card set	12
The Brass Teapot	2013 Wondercon	8 card set	15
The Creature Department	SDCC15	4 card set	8
The Elites	2014 Wondercon	4 card set	8
The Goldbergs	2015 D23	2 card set	15

Product Name	Convention/ Show Name	Description	Unit Price (USD)
The Ingredient	SDCC11	1 card	3
The Kane Chronicles	SDCC10	6 card set	5
The Mission	2014 Comikaze	1 card	5
The Muppets	Promotional	Fandom 9 card set UK only 100 sets	25
The Neighbors	2014 Wondercon	2 card set	10
The Nightsiders	SDCC15	6 card set	8
The Secret Series	SDCC12	6 card set	7
The Shadow of Oz	SDCC14	1 card	6
The Society	SDCC12	4 card set	10
The Spirit Movie		P-MS Exclusive Promo	10
The Super Newts	SDCC11	1 card	3
The Time Machine	SDCC01	5 card set	10
The Ultra Violets	SDCC13	4 card set	5
The Worlds End Movie cards	SDCC13	Set of 12 oversized cards	50
Titan Bookmarks	SDCC16	4 bookmark card set	25
Tmnt 2016 Movie	Promotional	4 card set	15
Toht New England	2015 Wondercon	1 card	4
Tom Cruise Oblivion	2013 Wondercon	3 card set	20
Toni Darling	SDCC14	2 card set	10
Tonner	SDCC14	3 card set	5
Top Trumps Dr Who Clara Oswold	SDCC13	1 card	25
Top Trumps Dr Who Abzorbaloff	SDCC09	1 promo card	10
Topps Abram Bazooka Joe	SDCC13	4 card set from book	15
Topps Celebration Set	2015 Star Wars Collection	100 card set	250
Topps Celebration Wrapper Set	2015 Star Wars Celebration	12 card set	35
Topps Garbage Pail Comic Connor	SDCC14	1 card	6
Topps Garbage Pail Puketacular and Fan Boyd	NYCC14	2 card set	8

Product Name	Convention/ Show Name	Description	Unit Price (USD)
Topps Mantic Mars Attacks Kickstarter Promo	2013 Comikaze	1 card	5
Topps Promo Card Set	SDCC08	13 card set	15
Topps Resistance Set	2016 Star Wars Celebration	6 card set	10
Topps Smilin Stan Garbage Pail Kids Promo Card	2014 Comikaze	1 card (standard size)	50
Topps Smilin Stan Garbage Pail Kids Promo Card	2014 Comikaze	1 oversized card	35
Topps Stan Strikes Mars Attacks Promo	2013 Comikaze	1 card	25
Topps Star Wars Card Trader Hans Solo	SDCC15	1 card	4
Topps Star Wars Card Trader Kylo Ren	NYCC	1 card	4
Topps Star Wars Daily Mail Set	Promotional UK	30 card set	30
Topps Star Wars Force Awakens	SDCC15	4 card set	100
Topps Star Wars Illustrated	2015 Star Wars Celebration	10 card set	25
Topps Star Wars Luke Skywalker	SDCC15	1 card	15
Topps Star Wars Rebels Set	2016 Star Wars Celebration	6 card set	10
Topps Wacky Packages Old Skull Promo	NYCC12	1 card	25
Toy Break	SDCC12	7 card set	20
Trade Skool	SDCC15	1 card	3
Trading Card Quest	2015 D23	30 card set. Various Disney characters	100
Trigger Armageddon	SDCC12	2 card set	6
Twilight	Promotional	2010 Holiday Exclusive Card. 500 made	10
Twilight	SDCC08	4 card set	50

Product Name	Convention/ Show Name	Description	Unit Price (USD)
Twilight	MEM08	P-MS Exclusive Promo	25
Twilight Breaking Dawn Part 2	SDCC12	15 card set	20
Twilight New Moon	SDCC09	10 card set	15
Twilight New Moon Burger King	Burger King	8 card set	10
Twilight Playing Cards	SDCC11	52 card set	50
Twistory	SDCC13	5 card set	15
Ultrasylvania	SDCC12	1 card	8
Ultrasylvania	2014 Wondercon	6 card set	15
Upper Deck Alien Legendary Encounters	SDCC14	1 card	5
Upper Deck Black Widow 3D	SDCC15	1 card	10
Upper Deck Iron Man 3D	SDCC15	1 card	15
Upper Deck JJ Kirby	SDCC16	1 card	25
Upper Deck Joe Jusko Marvel Masterpieces	SDCC14	2 card set	50
Upper Deck Marvel Gene X Patch	SDCC15	1 card	20
Upper Deck Marvel Patch Set	SDCC15	6 card set	75
Upper Deck Spiderman	SDCC09	1 card	10
Upper Deck Spiderman 3D	SDCC15	1 card	15
Upper Deck Spiderwoman	SDCC08	1 card	8
Vampirella	MEM12	2 card set	8
Vikings Ragner	SDCC13	1 card	10
Viz Tiger and Bunny	SDCC13	9 card set	15
Wacky Halloween	NYCC12	Topps Set of 7 postcards	55
Walking Dead S1	SDCC11	Rick Grimes promo cared	50
Walking Dead S2	SDCC12	1 card	5
Walking Dead S3	SDCC12	1 card	10

Product Name	Convention/ Show Name	Description	Unit Price (USD)
Wall-E	2015 D23	1 card	10
War of the Worlds	NEC UK	9 card preview set 2012	15
Warren the Ape	SDCC10	5 card set	25
Warrior Showdown	SDCC13	4 card set	15
Weaponeers of Monkaa	SDCC13	6 card set	15
Webble Cosplay	2013 Comikaze	22 card set	100
Webble Cospaint	2013 Comikaze	5 card insert set	100
Webble Series 2	SDCC14	1 card	4
William Shatner Stan Lee Set	SDCC16	4 card set	8
William Shatner Man O War	SDCC15	8 card set	16
Witches of East End	SDCC14	5 card set	100
Wookiepedia	2015 Star Wars Celebration	8 card set	10
World of Warcraft	2012 Wondercon	12 card set	10
Wrong Side of Normal	SDCC11	5 card set	25
X Files	SDCC08	XF SDCC Promo Card	10
X Men Apocalypse	SDCC15	4 card set	20
X Men Wolverine	SDCC09	8 card foil claw stamped set	75
Xenoglyphs	2012 Comikaze	2 card set	20
X Men Days of Future Past	SDCC14	1 card	6
X Men Carl's Jr.	Promotional	15 card set	20
Young & Hungry	2015 D23	2 card set	12
Zack's Ploitation	SDCC15	Unknown	50
Zen	SDCC11	1 card	3
Zombie	2014 Wondercon	6 card set	10
Zombie Outlaw	2011 Comikaze	1 card	5
Zombie Tramp	2016 Wondercon	1 card	3
Zombies	SDCC09	1 card	4
Zombies	SDCC13	5 card set	10
Zombies vs. Cheerleaders	Chicago Non Sports 2015	1 card	10
Zoolander 2 Promo	Edwards Irvine Cinema	1 card, only 200 made	5

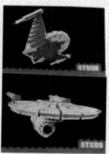

The Great Parking of the Droids

NOTES

NOTES

NOTES

NOTES

NOTES

NOTES

Made in the USA
Monee, IL
15 February 2021

60494024R00031